W9-AJT-557

Ladders

Weather

World Book

For information on other World Book products, call 1-800-WORLDBK (967-9325) or visit us at our Web site at http://www.worldbook.com

For information on sales to schools and libraries, call 1-800-975-3250.

Written by: Deborah Kespert
Story by: Sue Barraclough
Editor: Sarah Levete
Consultant: Barbara Taylor
Main illustrations: Fran Jordan
Computer illustrations: James Evans
Designer: Lisa Nutt
Art director: Belinda Webster
Pre-press production manager: Adam Wilde
Picture researcher: Jenny West
U.S. editor: Sharon Nowakowski, World Book Publishing

First published in the United States and Canada by
World Book, Inc.
233 N. Michigan Ave.
Chicago, IL 60601
in association with Two-Can Publishing Ltd.

© Two-Can Publishing 1999

All rights reserved. No part of this publication may be reproduced, stored in a retrieval system, or transmitted in any form or by any means electronic, mechanical, photocopying, recording, or otherwise, without written permission of the copyright owner.

"Two-Can" is a trademark of Two-Can Publishing

ISBN: 7166-7719-9
LCN: 99-67037

Photographic credits: p4: Image Bank; p5: Tony Stone Images; p6: Tony Stone Images; p7: Telegraph Colour Library; p8: Tony Stone Images; p11: Tony Stone Images; p15: Still Pictures; p16: Two-Can Design; p17: Telegraph Colour Library; p18: Pictures Colour Library; p19: Retna; p20: Collections/Anthea Sieveking; p22 Tony Stone; p23: Bruce Coleman Ltd.

Printed in China

3 4 5 6 7 8 9 10 05 04 03 02

What's inside?

This book tells you about different types of weather. You can find out how the weather changes during the year and what happens to plants and animals through the seasons.

Clouds and rain

Look up at the sky! Can you see any clouds? Are they white and fluffy or dark and gloomy? Clouds are made up of tiny drops of water. The drops grow bigger and heavier until they fall to the ground. It's raining!

This gray **cloud** is full of water and has just burst open!

Splish, splash! Lots of **raindrops** fall onto your hat.

When it pours rain, **puddles** of water are left on the ground.

Fog is a type of cloud that touches the ground. On a foggy day, it's hard to see far in front of you.

It's a fact!

The rainiest place on Earth is a town in India. All of the rain that falls there in a year would cover a three-story building.

A **raincoat** keeps out the water. Inside, you stay cozy and dry.

This beautiful band of colors is called a rainbow. It appears when there is rain and sunshine at the same time.

This dog has **wet fur**, so it shakes itself dry. Watch out for the splashes!

Can you see the wavy **ripples** in the water?

Wind

You can't see the wind, but you can feel it on your skin. Sometimes, the wind feels warm, but at other times it's cold. These pictures show you what can happen on windy days.

A **gentle breeze** makes your socks and T-shirts flap about on the clothesline.

The wind is blowing hard enough to push this windsurfer across the choppy water.

Whoosh! In a **strong breeze**, these colorful kites soar high into the air.

Look out! A sudden **gust** of wind can turn your umbrella inside out!

A fierce wind called a tornado whirls around like a spinning top. It looks like a long funnel.

In a strong **gale,** the wind whistles through the trees. Leaves fly everywhere.

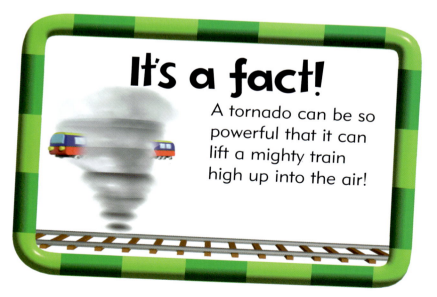

It's a fact!

A tornado can be so powerful that it can lift a mighty train high up into the air!

It's a storm!

When clouds in the sky loom big and dark, and the wind starts to howl, you know a storm is on the way. Suddenly, rain pours down. A storm can be exciting, but make sure you stay safely inside your home.

It's raining so hard that the road has started to **flood**.

A huge black **thundercloud** covers the sky.

Dazzling lightning is a giant spark of electricity from a thundercloud. It lights up the sky for a few seconds.

It's a fact!

During a storm, lumps of ice, called hailstones, may fall from the sky. The largest hailstones ever spotted were as big as tennis balls!

A flash of bright white **lightning** streaks through the sky.

Boom! If you see lightning, you will soon hear **thunder**.

❄ Snow and ice

On a cold day, snow falls from the sky and covers the ground like a white carpet. You can make funny shapes out of fresh, wet snow. If it's freezing cold, the snow may turn into hard, slippery ice.

Water in the clouds freezes into white **snowflakes** that fall gently to the ground.

It's a fact!

In some of the coldest parts of the world, people build shelters called igloos out of snow and slabs of ice.

A smiling **snowman** lasts for as long as the weather stays cold.

The wind blows the snow into a big pile called a **snowdrift**.

Long, sharp **icicles** are frozen drips of water or snow.

It's fun to make **footprints** in the crunchy snow!

Look at this delicate, lacy snowflake. Each tiny flake of snow has a different pattern.

Family snapshots

Take a look at the vacation photographs in our album. People take vacations come rain or shine!

Words you know

Here are some words that you read earlier in this book. Say them out loud, then try to find the things in the picture.

rainbow   raincoat
choppy water   puddles
thundercloud   snowflakes

What helps keep the girl dry in the rain?

What happens when it's sunny and rainy at the same time?

Changing Seasons

Some places have four seasons called spring, summer, autumn, and winter. Each season brings its own kind of weather. As the weather warms up and cools down, look out for all kinds of changes that happen.

spring

In spring, there are lots of **rain showers** and new flowers. The sun begins to shine more warmly, too.

It's a fact!

When it's winter and chilly in the top half of the world, it's summer and sunny in the bottom half of the world!

In winter, it may start to **snow**. This is the coldest time of year.

winter

In summer, the **sun** is high in the sky and shines brightly. This is the hottest time of year.

Some countries have only two seasons, one dry and one rainy. In the rainy season, it can pour for months!

In autumn, some **leaves** change colors and the days turn cooler.

Warm Spring

In spring, the weather warms up, and the days become longer. Now that the cold winter is over, plants push out of the ground and new leaves start to grow. Lots of baby animals are born, too.

Hundreds of tiny **buds** start to unfold.

The buds become bright green **new leaves**.

Gardeners are busy at this time of year. Gentle rain and warm sunshine help young plants to grow quickly.

Spring is a colorful season. The first **flowers** start to bloom.

A **baby lamb** has a thick woollen coat to keep it warm on cooler days.

A bird has returned from its winter home far away. It has built a snug **nest**.

The bird lays **eggs** in the nest. The eggs will hatch late in the spring.

These fluffy ducklings are a few weeks old. There is plenty of food to eat, so soon they will be big and strong.

Hot summer

In summer, the days are long and warm. It's fun to play outside when the sun shines brightly and the sky is blue. Insects buzz and flutter around gardens, which are packed with colorful, scented flowers.

The warm golden **sunshine** helps the flowers bloom.

Splashing in the **water** is a fun way to keep cool.

A striped bee lands on a flower. The bee collects a sweet juice called nectar.

A **sun hat** and sunglasses protect you from the sun's hot rays.

Never look directly at the sun. It could damage your eyes.

Make sure you rub plenty of sun block into your skin. It will help protect your skin from the strong sunshine.

The cat looks comfortable resting in the cool **shade**.

Bright **butterflies** flutter through the garden.

Cool autumn

On an autumn day, it's fresh and cool, even when the sun shines. Trees lose their leaves, fruit ripens, and animals prepare for the cold winter months. Early in the morning, the air may feel damp.

Colorful leaves fall from branches.

It's fun to **rake** the leaves that have fallen from the tree.

Juicy red apples are ready to be picked from the tree. This apple tastes sweet!

A **squirrel** collects nuts. It stores them, then eats them during the cold winter.

There are tasty **nuts** for animals to eat.

These **birds** are about to fly to a warmer place far away. They'll return in the spring.

It's a fact!

A squirrel hides nuts for the winter in all kinds of nooks and crannies, but sometimes it forgets where it has put them!

Cold winter

In winter, days are short, and nights are long. The sun's rays are weak and the weather turns cold. Many animals hide until the warm spring. Others are up and about during the cold weather.

There are many **bare trees** in winter. The leaves fell off the trees in autumn.

It's so cold that the water in this pond has frozen into **ice**.

This plant is covered in a coat of frost. It looks like icing on a cake!

Even in freezing winter, **pine trees** keep their leaves, called needles.

There's little food for birds to eat, except winter **berries**.

In the cold winter months, a dormouse sleeps in a cozy nest. It won't wake up until the warm spring arrives.

Seasons projects

Look at these colorful projects. They're perfect for keeping a record of changes through the seasons.

24

autumn

winter

How many fluttering butterflies can you count?

Words you know

Here are some words that you read earlier in this book. Say them out loud, then try to find the things in the picture.

bare trees   butterflies
nuts   berries
baby lamb   flowers

25

Grandma's amazing weather forecaster

WHAM, BANG, CRASH! As usual, mysterious noises were coming from Grandma's workshop…

Daisy just loved staying with her grandparents. She was especially excited because Grandpa had promised to take her to the safari park Saturday. Daisy couldn't wait to see the latest arrival, a fierce tiger!

The only thing that worried Daisy was Grandma's latest invention. Today, Grandma was busier than usual, tinkering in her workshop. "Daisy," said Grandma excitedly, "you'll never guess what I've invented."

"It's an amazing weather forecasting machine that will aways be right! I'm tired of the weather people being wrong. I know I can do better!" explained Grandma.

She pulled out a wrench and tweaked a huge dial on the front of the machine.

"Wait and see, Daisy, " said Grandma.

Wednesday, Daisy came down for breakfast and bumped into Grandma coming out of her workshop.

"It's going to snow today," warned Grandma. "We'll have to wrap up warmly to go shoppping." Daisy put on her coat, hat, and scarf and stepped outside into bright sunshine.

"Phew, it's hot! Are you sure it's going to snow, Grandma?" asked Daisy.

"Of course!" replied Grandma. "You'll be able to make a snowman after lunch."

As the summer morning wore on, Daisy grew hotter and hotter in her winter clothes.

"Hmmm," said Grandma thoughtfully. "My machine needs a little more work."

When they arrived home, Grandma disappeared into her workshop.

BANG! CRASH! SQUEAK! TWEAK!

"That should do it. My machine will get it right tomorrow," said Grandma.

Thursday morning was dark and gray, but Grandma was planning a picnic.

"Put on your shorts," she said confidently, "it will be warm and sunny."

"But Grandma," said Daisy, "look at those big thunderclouds."

"No buts, Daisy. The weather machine will be right." But by the time they reached the park, raindrops fell from the clouds. Soon it was pouring, and they all trudged home dripping wet.

"Never mind, Daisy," said Grandpa, "we'll have a great time at the safari park Saturday."

RUSTLE! RUMMAGE! SNAP! TAP!

"That should do it. My machine will get it right tomorrow," said Grandma.

That evening, Daisy found Grandma sorting out paint and paintbrushes.

"My weather forecasting machine says it will be calm and warm tomorrow," announced Grandma. "That's perfect weather to paint the shed."

Friday morning, Daisy and Grandma put on overalls and started to paint. Soon a strong breeze sent the clouds moving swiftly across the sky. Sudden gusts of wind sent the leaves swirling around. The leaves stuck to the shed, ruining Daisy and Grandma's careful work.

"It looks like the weather forecasting machine was wrong again!" moaned Daisy.

"Humph!" Grandma replied as she scurried back to her workshop.

SAW! GRIND! WHIRR! GRRRR!

"That should do it. My machine will get it right tomorrow," said Grandma.

Saturday morning, Daisy could hardly contain her excitement. Today she was going to the safari park to see a real tiger. Today would be great whatever the weather!

But Grandma was very concerned.

"My weather forecasting machine says a giant tornado is heading our way! I must warn everyone," she cried.

Daisy couldn't believe her ears.

"There's no way you can go outside. It's far too dangerous," Grandma said firmly.

Grandma knocked on every door on the street, telling everyone to stay inside with the doors and windows closed.

Soon the whole town was deserted. No children played in the gardens, no neighbors chatted over the fence. There was silence as everyone waited for the terrible tornado to arrive.

Suddenly a newsflash appeared on the television:

VERY URGENT WARNING! DANGEROUS TIGER ON THE LOOSE! STAY INSIDE WITH YOUR DOORS AND WINDOWS SHUT!

29

Daisy, Grandma, and Grandpa couldn't believe it. A mighty tiger was wandering down the empty street.

"Wow!" whispered Daisy. "A real tiger right outside the house!

The whole town watched with open mouths as the park rangers arrived. The rangers lured the tiger safely into a cage, then drove it back to the safari park.

People poured out of their houses, laughing and chatting. A crowd gathered outside Grandma's house and cheered as she opened her front door.

"How on earth did everyone manage to get indoors so quickly?" asked a reporter from the local paper.

"It was Daisy's grandma," said a boy. "She warned us about a t-t-t..."

"Tiger!" said Daisy quickly.

"Incredible!" said the reporter, scribbling in his notebook. "So Daisy's grandma saved the day!"

"Yes," laughed Daisy proudly, "she certainly did!"

Puzzles

Double trouble!

Look at these two pictures of a rainy day. Can you find four differences between picture a and picture b?

a

b

Close-up!

We've zoomed in on different kinds of weather. Can you guess what is in each picture?

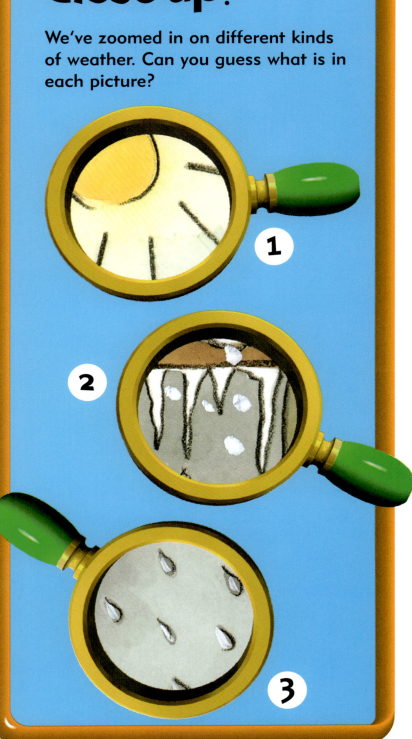

1

2

3

Answers: Double trouble! In picture b, the rainbow, splashes and one puddle are missing, the boots are purple. **Close-up!** 1 sun, 2 icicles, 3 raindrops.

True or false quiz

Can you figure out which of these statements are true? You can go to the page numbers listed to help you find out the answers.

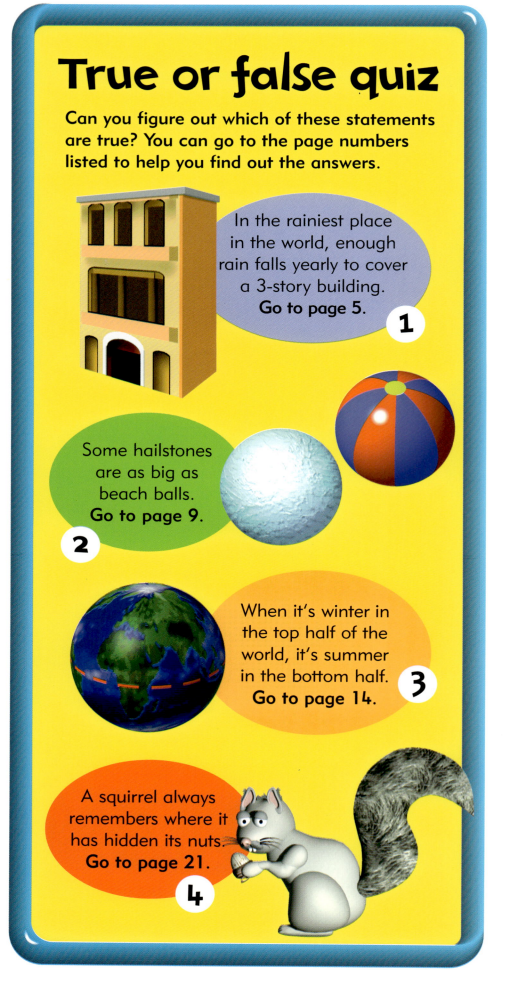

In the rainiest place in the world, enough rain falls yearly to cover a 3-story building. **Go to page 5.**

1

Some hailstones are as big as beach balls. **Go to page 9.**

2

When it's winter in the top half of the world, it's summer in the bottom half. **Go to page 14.**

3

A squirrel always remembers where it has hidden its nuts. **Go to page 21.**

4

Answers: 1 true, 2 false, 3 true, 4 false.

Index